T0052877

If you were a Verb?

by Michael Dahl
illustrated by Sara Gray

PICTURE WINDOW BOOKS
Minneapolis, Minnesota

verb (v or vb) a word that is used to express an action or condition

Editor: Christianne Jones
Designer: Nathan Gassman
Page Production: Tracy Kaehler
Creative Director: Keith Griffin
Editorial Director: Carol Jones
The illustrations in this book were created with acrylics.

Picture Window Books
1710 Roe Crest Drive
North Mankato, MN 56003
www.capstonepub.com

Copyright © 2006 by Picture Window Books, a Capstone imprint. All rights reserved. No part of this book may be reproduced without written permission from the publisher. The publisher takes no responsibility for the use of any of the materials or methods described in this book, nor for the products thereof.

Printed in the United States 4255

Looking for verbs?

Watch for the big, colorful words in the example sentences.

Special thanks to our advisers for their expertise:

Rosemary G. Palmer, Ph.D., Department of Literacy
College of Education, Boise State University

Susan Kesselring, M.A., Literacy Educator
Rosemount–Apple Valley–Eagan (Minnesota) School District

Library of Congress Cataloging-in-Publication Data
Dahl, Michael.
If you were a verb / by Michael Dahl ; illustrated by Sara Gray.
p. cm. — (Word fun)
ISBN 978-1-4048-1354-0 (hardcover)
ISBN 978-1-4048-1981-8 (paperback)
1. English language—Verb—Juvenile literature. I. Gray, Sara, ill.
II. Title. III. Series.

PE1271.D34 2006 2005021855
428.1—dc22

If you were a verb...

... you could SWIM,
DANCE,
TIPTOE,
LEAP,

PADDLE,
CARTWHEEL,
TRAVEL,
OR PLUNGE.

Verbs get things going!
If you were a verb, you could
BALANCE and BEND,
TWIST
and
TURN,

SWOOP and SOAR.

If you were a verb, you would appear in every sentence.

You would be in every book, every newspaper, every magazine, and every letter ever written.

If you were a verb,
you could be an action.
The mighty ship
SAILS out of the harbor.

Waves CRASH against its side.
Seagulls SCREAM overhead.

If you were a verb, extra words would help you show action. These extra words are called helping verbs.

You **MAY** give the usher your ticket now.

The popcorn **WILL BE** popping soon.

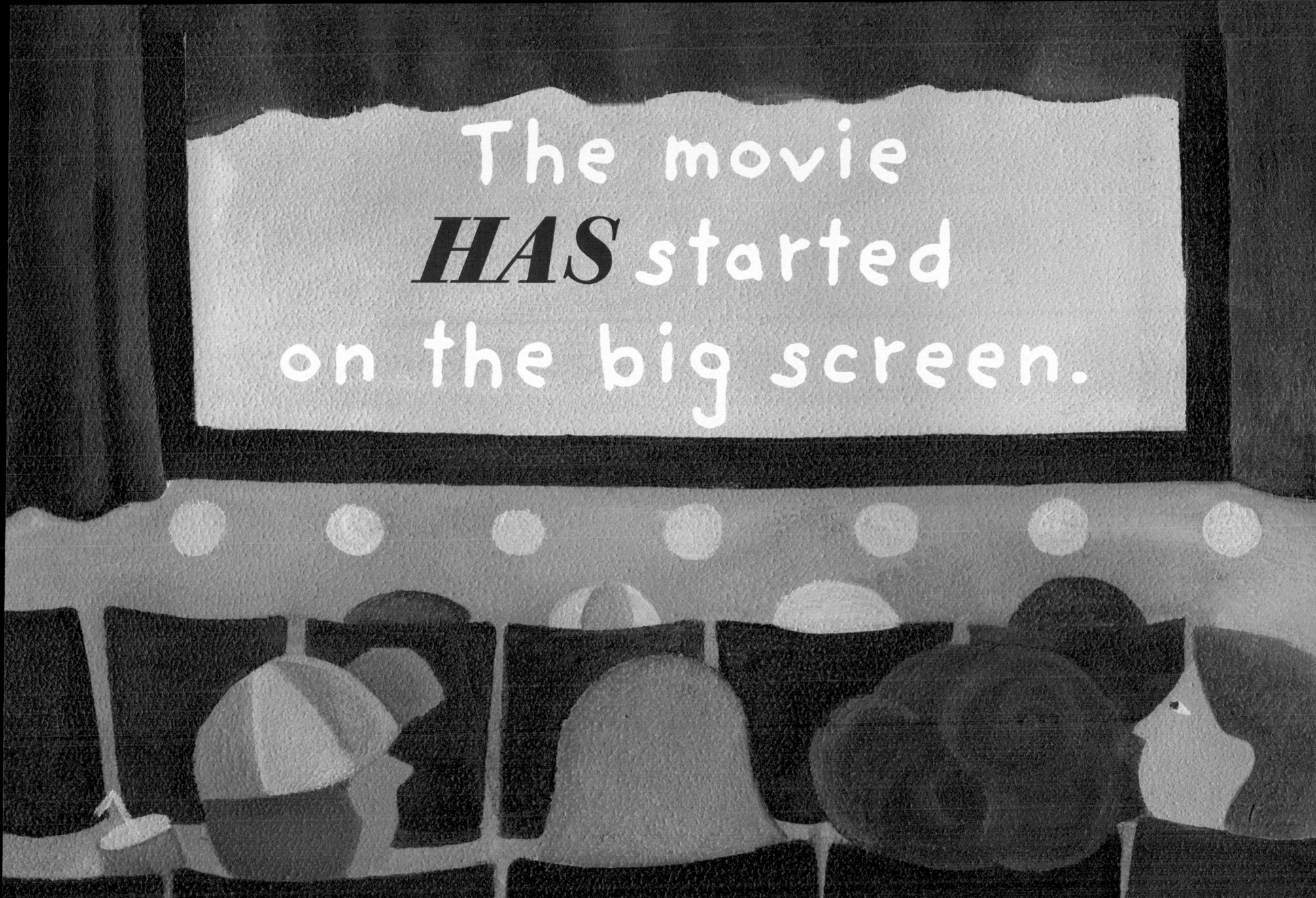

If you were a helping verb, you would have 23 members in your family: may, might, must, be, being, been, am, are, is, was, were, do, does, did, should, could, would, have, had, has, will, can, shall.

If you were a verb, you could link things together. You would be a linking verb. Sometimes linking verbs are called state-of-being verbs.
The swimmer WAS tired.
The beach ball IS floating.

The lifeguards
WERE done for the day.
If you were a linking verb, your
most common forms would be
is, am, were, was, are, be,
being, and been.

If you were a verb, you would change when time passed. You could be in past tense, present tense, or future tense.

Last night, the bicycles **GLIDED** through the park.

Now, the bicycles
GLIDE through the park.
Tomorrow, the bicycles
WILL GLIDE through the park.

If you were a verb, you would change when the number of people or things change.

One acrobat **SWINGS** above the crowd,

but five acrobats
SWING above
the crowd.

If you were a verb, you would get together with other verbs to make cool and exciting sentences.

The rocket **SPEEDS** toward the space station

that **WHIRLS**
and **SPINS** above Earth.

You could always be moving ...
... if you were a verb!

FUN with VERBS

Verbs can be full of action. Verbs can also be quiet.

Directions: Think of an action verb, such as running, jumping, or flying. Then make your friends guess what the verb is by acting it out. See how quickly they can figure out what your secret verb is. Take turns acting out action verbs and guessing.

Next, choose a quiet verb, such as standing, sleeping, thinking, staring, wishing, or hiding. Take turns acting out quiet verbs and guessing.

Is it harder to act out an action verb or a quiet verb?

Fact: If you look up a verb in the dictionary, you will see the abbreviation "v" or "vb" next to it. The "v" or "vb" stands for verb.

Glossary

acrobat—a person who performs stunts
glide—to move without any effort
harbor—a sheltered place along the coast where ships and boats anchor
soar—to fly high in the air
swoop—to go down suddenly
tiptoe—to walk quietly
usher—a person who leads people to their seats

To Learn More

At the Library

Cleary, Brian P. *To Root, to Toot, to Parachute: What Is a Verb?* Minneapolis, Minn.: Carolrhoda Books, 2001.
Heller, Ruth. *Kites Sail High: A Book About Verbs.* New York: Grosset & Dunlap, 1988.
Schneider, R. M. *Add It, Dip It, Fix It: A Book of Verbs.* Boston: Houghton Mifflin, 1995.

On the Web

FactHound offers a safe, fun way to find Internet sites related to this book. All of the sites on FactHound have been researched by our staff.

1. Visit *www.facthound.com*
2. Type in this special code: 1404813543
3. Click on the FETCH IT button.

Your trusty FactHound will fetch the best sites for you!

Index

changing shape, 18-19
changing with amounts, 18-19
changing with time, 16-17
types of verbs
  helping, 12-13
  linking (state-of-being), 14-15

Look for all of the books in the Word Fun series:

If You Were a Noun
If You Were a Verb
If You Were an Adjective
If You Were an Adverb
If You Were a Conjunction
If You Were an Interjection
If You Were a Preposition
If You Were a Pronoun
If You Were an Antonym
If You Were a Homonym or a Homophone
If You Were a Palindrome
If You Were a Synonym